101 Ways
to Make Guerrilla Beauty

Also by Trebbe Johnson:
The World Is a Waiting Lover

101 Ways to Make Guerrilla Beauty

Trebbe Johnson

RADJOY PRESS

Published in the United States by RADJOY PRESS,
a trademark of Vision Arrow

ISBN- 13 : 978-1545442739
ISBN- 10 : 1545442738

Design: Andrew B. Gardner

Manufactured in the United States

First Edition

Dedication

To all those who have made and will make beauty for the places on Earth that are going through hard times.

CONTENTS

– ONE –

What is Guerrilla Beauty?

What Is Guerrilla Beauty?

As the twenty-first century nears the end of its second decade, all of us citizens of the Earth find that we are forced to cope with challenges few could have imagined a generation ago. Even as global warming disrupts the seasons and fractures the weather patterns we've grown up with, most of us also deal on a daily basis with all-too-visible assaults on the beautiful wild places we love and the communities we live in.

Unfortunately, this trend shows no signs of improving. Many courageous people are working tirelessly to stave off the damage and create a sustainable, healthier environment for the future. Yet how can we possibly build the world we want if we ignore the places among us that that have been important and meaningful to us and now are broken, paved over, poisoned, or even gone forever?

Happily, there is one response to these large, seemingly unstoppable forces that any one of us can do at any time and in any place. It is a simple action that we can take regardless of age, race, religion, level of physical ability, or experience. It requires no training, unfolds without the need to haul in a bunch of supplies, and does not even demand advance preparation. It is both art and activism. You can do it alone, with a friend, or with a group. It empowers the individual, unites the community, and gives new life to places that have been given up as hopelessly lost.

This simple act is to make "guerrilla beauty" for the places you love that have been hurt.

The Spanish word *guerrilla* refers to warlike actions undertaken by small, independent groups of combatants in conflict with a large institutionalized military force. During the 1970s, for example, guerrilla forces in Nicaragua arose in an effort to overthrow a repressive and brutal government and establish new political institutions. Leftist Sandinistas harassed members of the wealthy, right-wing government, freed political prisoners, and launched ambushes against the army. In a non-warlike context, *guerrilla* has come to refer to actions undertaken by small bands of individuals, usually in impromptu ways and without authorization.

What the guerrilla beauty we propose here has in common with the original meaning is that it is spontaneous, bold, and anonymous. It is also intended to strike at what is wrong by using methods so unconventional that they attract the attention of other citizens, the media, and even corporate and government officials. Guerrilla beauty differs from guerrilla war, however, because it is non-confrontational, compassionate, and always creative, rather than destructive.

Guerrilla beauty is also different from other forms of art and environmental activism. You offer guerrilla beauty to a place that matters to you without expectation of payment, fame, or even thanks. Every person who is present pitches in. Moreover, you and your fellow humans are only the first creators of this art. Wind, rain, animals, and even traffic will continue to dabble with what you've made after (or even during) the time you're working.

Making beauty of this kind serves the people who make it, but the ultimate recipient is the place itself. The places we love that are under assault have given a great deal of themselves. They offer habitat, clean water for people and animals and plants, fertile soil, beauty, wood for fires and building, a source of spiritual wonder, and countless other gifts. Now they are struggling. We offer each simple act of beauty to a place as a gift. It may be a gift given in gratitude for what the place has bestowed so generously on others, both human and non-human, or it may be a gift of consolation for what the place is suffering now.

Giving a gift of guerrilla beauty is also motivated by an impulse that differs from most acts of art or charity or ecology. Although you may also be motivated to take this action in order to rebuild a community, encourage creativity in a local population, motivate people to stay true to a struggle, raise awareness, or some other intention, those reasons are secondary. The primary reason for making this gift is out of a shared love for the place.

There are many ways to make guerrilla beauty. The pathway described in this book is known as the Earth Exchange. It is a simple practice founded by Radical Joy for Hard Times, and it entails five suggested steps:

1. Meet with friends at a wounded place
2. Sit awhile and share your stories
3. Get to know the place as it is now
4. Share what you discovered
5. Make a Gift of Beauty

Every year Radical Joy for Hard Times sponsors the Global Earth Exchange, a day in June when people all over the world go to wounded places and make beauty in the form of a bird made of materials the place itself provides. We also offer special programs for our global network and in local communities. The Ground Beneath Our Hearts in 2015 was a day of art and music that unfolded in ten communities, from Azerbaijan to the California desert, where mineral extraction is causing severe hardship to people. For Gulf Coast Rising in 2010, people hurt by the BP oil leak shared acts of generosity with one another and the land.

People who have participated in or heard about these powerful events have often asked us for suggestions on how to create beauty for wounded places and also for how to keep the momentum going after the event is over. In response, we offer this book, *101 Ways to Make Guerrilla Beauty.* It contains concrete ideas about how to make simple acts of creative, spontaneous guerrilla beauty for a wide variety of hurt or endangered places.

The book is divided into eight chapters. Chapters 1-4 are devoted to the corresponding steps of the Earth Exchange. Chapters 5-7 elaborate on the most important step, which is the making of your gift of beauty for the place. Chapter 5 offers suggestions that you can use in a variety of different places and circumstances. Chapter 6 spotlights specific kinds of wounded places and practices that work particularly well in them. Chapter 7 has ideas for how to keep the momentum of your Earth Exchange going through return visits and other activities. Chapter 8 broadens the concept of making beauty for wounded places to show how it is relevant to all kinds of life situations.

You're welcome to read this book from cover to cover, jump right to the section you're most interested in, or skim. We invite you to turn to *101 Ways of Making Guerrilla Beauty* repeatedly for ideas, inspiration, and reflection. And please send us the stories and photographs of your own Earth Exchanges. You never know how they might end up motivating others!

– TWO –

The
Earth Exchange

1—

MEET WITH FRIENDS
AT A WOUNDED PLACE

The first step of an Earth Exchange is to go to the wounded place. Being there in person, on the land or by the water, grounding yourself in the place that has fallen on hard times is very important. It's fine to meditate on a hurt place from afar, but that's not an Earth Exchange. Focusing on the place in your mind—or even in your heart—just maintains your separation from it. And of course, all too often, distancing is exactly the response so many of us revert to when a place is damaged or destroyed. It's no longer what it used to be or what we wish it were, so we ignore it. It becomes, in the words of Middlebury College professor and author Adrian Ivakhiv, "taboo." It's off limits, officially or in the minds of people or both.

So the point of the Earth Exchange is to move out of our comfort zone and actually make a visit to this place. Think of it as a *pilgrimage*, a spiritual journey made with a mission. Your mission on this Earth Exchange pilgrimage is to become reacquainted with a place that is being neglected, ignored, forgotten. You go there to find out how it's doing in its current state and also to be open to how *you're* doing. You don't have to fix anything. You don't have to convert anyone. Your mission is not to heal either the place or the people. You're simply there to find and make a little beauty.

Don't worry if you feel anxiety or trepidation before you set out. Whatever you feel when you begin is likely to change into something else. You will be surprised. You will notice things you did not expect to notice and feel things you did not expect to feel.

Although this step says to "meet with friends," it's also fine if you go to a wounded place alone. A big part of why the Earth Exchange works is that any person can do it at any time in any place. You can plan weeks ahead for your event or you can do it on the spur of the moment whenever the need of a place and your own inclination seize you.

No matter where you go or with how many people, it is essential that you insure the health and safety of yourself and everyone else. Avoid places where the land is unstable, such as the sites of explosions, earthquakes, or rock slides. Do not expose yourself and your group to toxic waste or pollution. (If you want to do an Earth Exchange for a toxic place, see pages 63-64). Don't break laws or trespass.

The following suggestions will guide you into your first few moments of being at a wounded place.

When you come to a wounded place that makes you feel sad, don't just walk or drive on. Risk the encounter! If you're driving, get out of the car. If you're walking, pause. Face the place and take it in. Note the details. What are the boundaries of this wounded place? Is there an epicenter, where the situation looks and feels worse than in other places? Note how you are feeling about witnessing what has happened or is happening. Acknowledge that your feelings confirm your connection with this place. Even if you pause for just a moment or two, you have begun to bridge the gap between a place that has fallen on hard times and the humans who can care for it.

When you are ready to enter your wounded place, step over a "threshold." Before you and those who are with you step onto the grounds of the place you've chosen, make a simple threshold. It can be a line drawn in the soil, a stick, a row of stones, a branch, or other clear boundary line. Stepping mindfully over a demarcation between the world you typically inhabit and this place that has become separate from other, healthier places transforms your presence there from a mere visit into an event filled with meaning and import. The place becomes what the Greeks called a *temenos*, a space set aside from common use and dedicated to sacred activities. Stepping over a threshold also enables you to regard your own presence there as sacred and meaningful.

When your Earth Exchange is complete, step back over the threshold.

Move more slowly than you think you need to. When you first arrive at this wounded place, you may be tempted to proceed quickly through the steps of the Earth Exchange in order to get it over with quickly, so you can leave. Acknowledge this impulse—and then do your best to resist it. You are here to visit this place as if it were a sick friend (which it is), get to know it, and let it get to know you. So, instead of hurrying, try moving with exaggerated slowness.

Don't run away—from the place or yourself. Whatever you feel, it will shift in a moment. Your feelings won't destroy you. What usually happens, in fact, is that opening up to them has just the opposite effect: after a moment of intensity, the first burst of feeling passes and shifts into something else. You may even feel a sense of relief. You have faced what you did not want to face, and now you are available to new feelings such as compassion, courage, and a greater sense of connection to all life.

11

Practice balance (Part A). If you find that conflicting emotions are swirling within you, don't try to choose between them. Acknowledge these opposites. They may be sorrow and fascination, anger and admiration, delight and despair, anger and hopelessness, or anything else. Imagine that you can hold these emotions gently in each of your hands. Recognizing that both are true for you in this instant means that you are able to open up to the widest possible state of presence within yourself.

Have fun. The place, the community, the nation, the world—there is plenty of sadness all around. Making a gift of beauty for a place you love and getting reacquainted with it in the process ought to provide some joy. Stephen Duncombe, founder of Creative Activism and author of *Dream: Re-imagining Progressive Politics in an Age of Fantasy,* writes: "If progressives hope to appeal to anyone outside of a small group of self-flagellants and the terminally self-righteous, we need to cultivate and articulate positive associations with progressive politics."[1] So let yourself have fun.

2—

SIT AWHILE AND SHARE YOUR STORIES

Taking a few minutes for everyone in the group to share their personal feelings and experiences about the place helps to strengthen the bond between individuals and the place. When your group has gathered at the place you've chosen, sit or stand in a circle.

Now ask each person to introduce themselves and talk briefly about their relationship to the place or the species you've come to honor, both before and after it came to be in its present condition. Every one of us has a personal connection with the natural world we live in. Sometimes we are connected to places because their beauty (or former beauty) has touched us. Sometimes we have special memories of the place that now re-emerge. Sometimes we realize that we have paid scarcely any attention at all to the place for years, but now that it is endangered we suddenly feel a rush of attachment to it. Feelings of love, awe, delight, and wonder that we felt in the past about a place continue to affect us, even after that place has been radically changed.

For some people, this may be the first time they have ever actually visited this place. They can simply express their feelings about being there now. Maybe the place reminds them of some other experience of loss or damage in their life. A woman who went with friends to do an Earth Exchange at the endangered Susquehanna River in Binghamton, New York talked in this first circle of how her brother had drowned in a flooded river in Vermont and how the Susquehanna on a sunny day reminded her that rivers have many moods.

Here are a few suggestions for sharing your personal stories:

Be patient with one another. Not everyone responds to a wounded place in the same way. The person you're with might speak more quickly or deliberately or mindfully or playfully or casually or solemnly than you do.

Share your stories in a Council format. Choose a stick or stone from the place, or bring an object from home that you can pass around from one person to another as people speak. While each person holds this object, they are the center. They may speak from the heart without being interrupted, questioned, or asked for explanation.

Being able to speak in this way, so different from how we can usually express ourselves, is very freeing. You are able to plunge deeply into your own emotions, memories, thoughts without any anxiety about being judged. When each person is finished, they pass the "talking object" to the person on their left, and the process continues until everyone has spoken. You might want to set guidelines in the beginning for how long each person speaks, reminding the group that everyone will have a turn.[2]

Relax! No one has to be in control of the situation. You are just the initiator of this event. Each person present will relate to the place in his or her own way. Think of it this way: your primary job is simply to introduce the people and the place to one another, and then step back, so they can get to know each other!

Let words be stories. If there isn't time or space, or if the circumstances simply aren't right for people to share their personal stories at first, ask everyone present to think of five words that describe their feelings upon entering this place. Then go round the circle so each person can express their five words.

3—

GET TO KNOW THE
PLACE AS IT IS NOW

After everyone has shared their feelings about the wounded place, take some time to get to know it as it is now. This part of the process is a mindful deepening into the kind of dialogue with the world that we all carry on unconsciously every single day. In any encounter with any landscape—including any cityscape—outer impressions and events interweave with our own personal histories, interests, and imaginations. The world around us reflects our inner self, and the inner self responds, which then shifts our perception of the outer world. It is an ongoing, usually unconscious process. With the Earth Exchange, we simply bring the whole thing into awareness.

Sometimes people who go to wounded places feel uncomfortable about being there and are eager to leave, so they hurry to find beauty and get away as soon as possible. Their haste prevents them from taking in what's really there, what really wants to grab their attention. It is important to allow the place to reveal itself to you slowly, gradually, just as a new friend would reveal aspects of her life and concerns over time, rather than all at once.

One way to enter into this experience of getting-to-know is simply by *gazing*. Gazing is a way of opening up to the living, present reality of a person, place, or object without any urgent insistence on results. When you gaze, you let yourself absorb the whole environment and note how the details emerge in their own time. Another way of thinking about this process is to imagine that certain aspects of the place are "calling to you." In other words, you look around until some particular feature draws your attention, and then you focus on that for awhile until something else calls. You can sit still to practice your gazing, you can walk around, or you can use a combination of both. The most important thing is to be curious and open to discovery.

Even if you are already very familiar with this place, be assured that it has plenty of surprises in store for you. Places, like people, are constantly changing. Here are some suggestions for how to absorb and be absorbed by your place:

Allow yourself to be distracted—but only by what's around you, not by your cell phone or your to-do list. Let your attention roam and when it finds something to settle on, let it settle. When it wants to roam, let it roam.

Move around as if all features of this place are as curious about you as you are about them. Opening your imagination to the possibility that everything in this place is alive can shift the way you perceive it and relate to it. Rather than being a member of a package tour with a few scant moments to glance at a famous monument, you become an explorer in a magical land.

Give voice to your emotions. If you're angry, shout. If you're sad, weep. If you're mixed up and unsure what you feel, try articulating that feeling by stammering, bleating, or gasping. Express your emotions out loud. Words and sounds can help difficult feelings to move through you, so you don't feel trapped in them. If you hear other people from the group expressing their own feelings out loud, just let them be.

Express your emotions with your body. Besides using your voice to express what you feel about being at this place, use your body as well. Stand on something and sing, throw something, bathe in clean water, hug a tree or the post of the front porch of a historic house that's about to be demolished so a high-rise can take its place. Do a dance. Lie on the ground. Your body knows exactly how to put emotions into movement.

Look for what's hurt. Look for what's beautiful. One way to practice balance in your attitude is to explore balance in the place. Go off on your own, away from the group, and look for something that disturbs you. Spend a minute or two with it. Then look for something that makes you happy or eases your tension. Spend a minute or two with it. Again find something that disturbs you, then something you are pleased to see. Go back and forth like this, alternating between what you like looking at and don't like looking at. Make an effort to spend equal amounts of time with both the sad and the joyful, the beautiful and the not-beautiful, the disturbing and the comforting. As you do so, you are improving your inner balance and gaining strength to cope not just with this place, but also with other highs and lows of life.

Look at this place with your imagination, not your intellect. If a tree reminds you of a dragon, let it be a dragon. If you feel sorry for a river because it seems to be suffering from all the poisons that have spilled into it, don't try to be reasonable and convince yourself that rivers don't have feelings. Grieve for the river. Your presence in this wounded place is a special occasion. Therefore, special ways of perceiving, which we all excelled at as children, are entirely appropriate and help us become more attuned to the ongoing aliveness of the place.

Learn how your place is part of the whole Earth. When you begin your practice of attending to this place, you may see only what's wrong with it. After you have taken as much time as you need to look at and consider the wounded aspect of it, let your gaze move wider afield. Turn around and look into each of the four directions. Gaze far into the distance and then switch your attention to the ground right in front of your feet. Continue the practice by moving slowly in a circle. Consider how your place is part of the whole community, the whole region, the whole Earth.

Notice what you are called to pay attention and what you wish to avoid. Do you turn away from looking at or stepping into certain areas? Are there other areas where you long to spend some time? Notice your inclinations, but do not judge them. You may or may not follow these impulses to approach one thing or move away from another. But be aware of them, for they have much to teach you about how you respond to your world.

Allow yourself to be "disarranged". Francis Ponge, the French poet and chronicler of the mythic existence of ordinary things, believed that the only way to really see the world was to let it "disarrange" you. Becoming disarranged engages you in regarding the infinite things and beings of the world not as inferiors that you must somehow corral for your own use and understanding, but as equals capable of amazing you as they reveal the facets of their particular selfhood.[3]

Walk the edges. Where does the wounding of this place begin and where does it end? Try to locate the borderline where the woundedness meets the whole. Practice crossing back and forth from one to the other. Do this slowly and attentively, paying attention to how you feel as you leave one area and enter the other. Note how your feelings about this back-and-forth movement change the more you experiment with it.

Gaze with meditative expectation, as if something surprising could reveal itself at any minute. It will.

Let go of the need to see something amazing. Even as you open your eyes and your expectations to what's around you in this place, don't feel you have to discover an incredible sight or sound or symbol. This journey is not about having an experience you can tell your friends about, something that will make it all worthwhile. It's all about bringing your attention to a place and receiving what the place has to show and tell you—and only you.

Gaze patiently. You may find that, after a moment or two, your mind thinks you've spent enough time regarding this particular tree or stone or landfill and that now you must move on. When that happens (*when*, not *if*), allow your attention to plunge in once again to where you are at that moment, like a swimmer diving into a deep pool. Focus on that particular thing for another few minutes. And perhaps another few minutes after that.

Get acquainted with both your hawk and your mouse vantage points. As you get to know your place, you are like a mouse. As a little creature, you are immediately and closely engaged in the land around you. Its smells, sights, and sounds are of vital importance to you, and you follow your nose in tracking them or quite deliberately staying clear of them. You are also like the hawk. You have an overview. You observe with curiosity what the mouse is doing—where she's drawn, what she wants to avoid, what obstacles she comes across, where she pauses—but you do not pounce and snatch her out of her terrain. You circle around, observing the whole. You act—and you observe your-self acting.

Don't try to fix anything. Remind yourself that this visit to your place doesn't have to produce any measurable results. You don't have to fix anything. You don't have to pull weeds or tidy up or even, at this stage of the journey, pick up trash. You also don't have to figure out what agency or expert needs to come in and start putting things to rights. It's fine if you return to these considerations later on, but for now, just be present.

Gaze with your memory. If you're in a wounded place and you're suddenly seized by a thought of a wounded place in your own life, acknowledge it. Sometimes people assume that their only purpose here must be to give attention to the place and push their personal life into the background. Repairing and restoring the relationship between people and place means *letting the place into your heart.* Once that happens, once the physical place you're standing in finds room in your heart, memories nudged by your current experience tend to emerge.

So if you find yourself revisited by a current or former place of suffering, let the wounded place you're in witness you, as you witness it. Let the crumbling stone wall stand for the family structure that crumbled during your childhood. Let the dried and dessicated riverbed draw you back to the weakness and depletion you felt after a relationship ended. Talk to the wounded place about what you're remembering. Talk out loud. Doing so can bring you relief as it brings you closer to the wounded place you're in.

On a visit to a Virginia forest that had burned in a wildfire, Carolyn Lyday was drawn to a sapling tree. The tree was badly charred, likely dead, and her heart swelled with pity for it. As she gazed at the black, cracked bark and considered how the tree had been consumed by fire before it could grow to maturity, she thought of her sister. She, too, was undergoing a kind of burning at that time as she underwent radiation treatments for breast cancer. Carolyn's sorrow about the violence the tree had undergone crested into grief for what her sister was suffering. She wept for both. Then she put her arms around the tree and sang it a lullaby that her mother had sung to her and her sister when they were small.

Be in this place not as an expert in your field but as a novice sitting at the feet of a marvelous teacher. Nature is a great teacher who always has something to show us about herself and about us as well, if only we are willing to pay attention. None of us ever has so many impressive credentials that we can't learn more from her.

4—

SHARE STORIES OF
WHAT YOU DISCOVERED

After everyone has spent time alone getting to know the place, it's a good idea to gather again in a circle, so people can share what they discovered.

This part of the Earth Exchange is often done as a Council (see page 14). The Council practice, in which the one who holds the talking object (a stick or stone, for example), "has the floor" is much different from how we typically communicate. It is both comforting and freeing to know that whatever you say will not be interrupted, that your words will be met with silent attention and respect. That is especially important after people have spent time alone in the place, as emotions can be vulnerable, edgy, and sensitive.

Occasionally, when people return to the group after their time alone with the place, they dismiss their experience. "Nothing happened," they say off-handedly.

Something always happens! When any person goes into any place, they bring their whole life experience, their desires, their fears, their fondness for certain colors and landscapes and their dislike of others. They also bring their current mood about what they have been dealing with during that particular day. The place, meanwhile, meets each person with its own particular "selfness"—the details of what happened to it, the lay of the land, the weather, the presence of animals and other people. Together, person and place have an encounter—and something always happens.

Telling stories of how each person present has seen, felt, explored, and discovered the place as it is now makes an impact on everyone. Whether it's two friends or a whole group, this second opportunity for storytelling weaves all those present into the awareness that the kinship between people and place never stops, no matter what has happened to the place. Someone shares that he found a sunflower growing out of a pile of debris in a neighborhood shattered by a tornado. Someone sat on a log in an old-grown clear-cut and wondered how the loggers felt when they cut those ancient trees. Someone prayed for the fish and other aquatic creatures killed when a chemical spill turned a river orange. Each of these stories brings new life into what was previously considered a place devoid of life and value and possibility. All together the stories revive the place and revive the way the people think about it.

In addition to the suggestions in Chapter 2 about telling and hearing stories, here are a few more, specifically related to this particular part of the visit:

When stories are shared, they intersect, or seem to. You never know when you will hear part of your story in another person's narrative. Suddenly, you recall that you, too, saw a certain sight or heard a sound at this place. At the time it slipped past your awareness, and now it rises up to show itself more forcefully, giving you new insight into what you yourself experienced. Each layer of each story reveals another in the limitless, interconnected strands of unfolding life in a place and the people who attend to it.

Together all the stories weave a physical, social, and psychological fabric of reality about the place. Each story is unique and each is part of all the others.

Each person's story is complete just as it is. It needs no embellishment, no corrections, no suggestions from others on how it might have been different, longer, more emotional, less detailed. It requires no fact-checking. For some people, especially those with expertise about the place or the event that damaged it, resisting the urge to correct others may be a challenge. What's important is not accuracy but how each person opened up to the life of the place.

When all members of the group have finished sharing their experiences, invite everyone to sit in silence for a moment and let the stories wash over them like a gentle rain. Imagine these stories nourishing the wounded place and reviving it.

– THREE –

101 WAYS
TO MAKE
GUERRILLA BEAUTY

5—

MAKE A GIFT OF GUERRILLA BEAUTY FOR YOUR WOUNDED PLACE

The part of the Earth Exchange that most profoundly alters people's attitudes about a wounded place—and even seems to shift the energy in the place itself—is the making of a gift of beauty. Think of it this way: For a long time, maybe even thousands or millions of years, the place has given abundantly of itself, not only to you and other humans, but to the countless non-human living creatures who have inhabited it, moved through it, and relied on it. It has provided branches to nest in, a vista of rippling green hills to enchant the eye, an architectural complex of coral for fish to feed on or hide in. And now, after such generosity, the place can give no more. At the very least, it cannot give what it used to give.

Your mission in this step of the Earth Exchange is to give something back. Your gift is not expensive. It's not even practical, like a clean-up or restoration. It is simply an expression of gratitude or appreciation or consolation, a living work of art made of and for one particular place on Earth by one particular group of people at one particular moment in time. It is an offering that represents both the condition of the place and the response of you and the others who love it. It requires no outside materials, no expertise, no prior experience. The place you are honoring with your gift has been abused and neglected. Your very presence there and now this gift you make reverse that pattern.

Depending on the place and the mood of the people, your gift might be solemn or whimsical, exuberant or thoughtful. It might take you five minutes or five days to complete. Whatever the gift ends up being, it is essential that everyone present participate in the activity, no matter their age, level of physical ability, protests that someone "isn't artistic," or any other obstacle. When everyone gets involved, they contribute to reinforcing the message that this place is important to many, that everyone who is present has a stake in it and is an intrinsic part of it still.

Working together to make this gift, you transform injury into imagination, neglect into care, sorrow into joy. Guided by the place itself, you usher yourselves into new territory, where you become creators, adventurers, takers of risk, generous givers, and bestowers of beauty. In the process you guide one of the wounded places of the Earth back into the circle of life. As the poet Galway Kinnell once put it, you "reteach a thing its loveliness."

The effect of making this gift is often very powerful for those present. People comment that a place that seemed ugly and useless to them when they arrived now seems to be full of beauty and resilience. Many have remarked in amazement that they feel love for a place they may have been avoiding for months or even years. They are empowered to use this simple but profound action as the springboard for other actions, a new way of involving themselves in the ongoing care and restoration of the place. "The land felt dead when we arrived," said one woman. "Afterwards, it felt alive. We were sad to leave."

Make your act of guerrilla beauty for this place not to change the world, or even to change the place, but as an act of love. Do it so that what's wrong won't change you. A.J. Muste was a Dutch-born pacifist and anti-war activist who made a practice of going every night during the Vietnam war to the front gate of the White House, where he would light a candle. One night a reporter asked him, "Mr. Muste, do you really think you are going to change the policies of this country by standing out here alone at night with a candle?" Muste allegedly replied, "Oh, I don't do it to change the country, I do it so the country won't change me."

We go to the places we love and mourn because we cannot create a better future until we heal our relationship with where we are right here and right now. And making a gift of beauty is a first vital and very empowering step to doing so.

Chapters 5-7 of this book present 101 ways of making guerrilla beauty for places. In this chapter you'll find general suggestions that you can apply to many different kinds of places, no matter what condition they're in or what kind of wound they may have:

1. Make the RadJoy bird. Every year in June, Radical Joy for Hard Times holds a Global Earth Exchange, when people all over the world go to wounded places they care about and make a bird—the RadJoy Bird—as their gift of beauty. We craft a bird because every place in the world has birds, and they are universal symbols of transcendence and freedom. Also, like RadJoy communities, they keep on singing, even through the worst of times. People have made birds of seashells, stones, the limbs of cut trees, trash, pine cones, drawings in the sand, their own bodies, and many other "art supplies" that the place offered them.

2. Make sound. Nothing fires up group energy and resonates through the air like a joyful noise! You don't even have to come prepared with a drum or musical instrument. You can strike two stones or two sticks together, clap your hands, sing, and make sounds you've never made before that the place inspires. Open up and don't be concerned about doing it right! Have everyone make their own sounds at first and then see if and how they all come together.

3. Make something the place needs. If your place it wounded, it's missing something it once had, something that used to thrive here. What is that missing element? Frogs that vanished after a wetland was drained to make way for a mall? The peak of a mountain flattened by a coal mining company? Maybe it's the children who used to play here and can no longer do so. Give your wounded place a symbolic offering of what it's lost. Gather materials that the place provides: pine cones, stones, flowers, sand. Work together, with everyone adding pieces to the image. In a drought-stricken forest near Perth, Australia, Glenn Albrecht found several brilliant tail feathers of the forest red-tailed black cockatoo, which is endangered because its habitat is dying. He arranged them in a fan shape and placed them in the notch of a dead tree.

4. Read the place a story. When you arrive for your Earth Exchange, bring along a poem or story about what the place used to be like before it was hurt. Take turns reading this piece aloud, everyone reading a paragraph or so. Read not to one another, the human members of the group, but to the life forces of the place itself.

5. Make offerings. An offering, in the spiritual context, is a gift or contribution that is typically made to a god or divine being. It is a way of "feeding" this being with appreciation, devotion, and gratitude. You can feed the depleted spirit of your place as well. Iris Weaver led a group in making an offering not just to the Atlantic Ocean off the coast of Massachusetts, but to all the oceans of the Earth. First they called in the spirit of Mother Ocean and asked her to hear their prayers and receive their gifts. Then everyone addressed the ocean and told her what she meant to them. As they did so they presented their offerings of flowers, stones, shells, or other special objects by tossing them into the surf. They concluded their ceremony by reading a prayer for healing the ocean and all waters.

6. Make a group offering. Another option for creating an offering to a place is for everyone present to construct it together and then present it to its recipient. A group at the opposite side of the United States from Iris and her group did this for the Pacific Ocean. On a large, round tray they created a mandala of sand, flowers, honey, tobacco, and other organic elements. As they worked, each person expressed what she or he loved about the ocean and what grieved them about the pollution, trash, and warming trends threatening it. When they were finished, they walked together to the shoreline and poured the offering into the surf. They stood and watched as the waves hungrily consumed the offering.

7. Play house. Imagine that this place is a new home you're moving into. How would you like to decorate it? Are there branches or rocks where your friends will sit when they come to visit? Does a dining room present itself? A bedroom? A playroom for the children? What natural or human-made objects can you move around to make the place cozy and inviting? After you've got things arranged to your liking, borrow a practice from your childhood self and have a make-believe tea party.

8. Comfort this place. When we're hurt, what we often want is not advice or solutions as much as simple comfort. We want others who care about us to recognize our suffering and treat us with compassion. Maybe hurt places would appreciate such treatment as well! Encourage everyone in the group to go in their own direction and offer comfort to this place. Your expression of comfort could be gentle words such as, "There, there" or

"You'll be all right" or "I know it hurts." Or you can gently caress the ones that dwell in this place—the grasses, the tree stumps, the soil, even the inanimate ones like fences, piers, or signposts. You may find that as you do this simple practice, greater and deeper levels of compassion wash over you.

9. Do a ceremony. Ceremony is a process of moving mindfully and symbolically from one state of being to another. Actions and words that we make within the limited time and particular space of the ceremony symbolize our intention to live a certain way in the world over a span of unlimited time and unbounded space. Think of a wedding: two individuals come together before family and friends and express their commitment to creating a life together. They communicate this desire through an exchange of vows, by the way they approach the person who is officiating (often approaching separately and meeting together before the assembled guests), placing rings on each other's fingers, and sealing the bond with a kiss. Each ceremony enacts a path for stepping from the present into the future.

To create your own ceremony, decide what state of being you will start with and what you will end with. You might choose a kind of "wedding" or ceremony of commitment to the place; a ritual to remember people, animals, or trees that lost their lives there; or a simple ceremony of hope that a damaged place can once again become whole. A group of children in Chicago led an event like that at Lake Michigan. Standing at the shoreline, each child dipped a cup into the polluted lake and filled it with water. They then held the cups to their hearts, offered the water their love, and poured the water back.

Pay attention to what may happen during your ceremony! Even if you have an idea of the beginning and the end, you may be surprised by what happens in the middle. Be attuned to the energy of the group, your own emotions and intuition, and anything you may encounter, such as a wind, a wave, traffic, or a passerby. Instead of being a disruption, it might just play an important part in what's unfolding here.

10. Make a mandorla to inhabit the place where grief and joy meet. The mandorla is a living symbol that can help to unify two seemingly contrary aspects of ourselves. You can see a mandorla in the almond-shaped segment where two circles overlap. It originated as a medieval Christian symbol that depicted the separate spheres of heaven and earth and the meeting place between them that is the human heart. Psychologist Robert Johnson has written that, by inhabiting each circle in turn, or each side of two opposing constellations of our being, and then spending time in the place where the opposites join, we discover wholeness.[4]

For this act of beauty, create two circles on the ground in your wounded place using rope, string, or materials found on site. Make sure each circle is large enough that it is possible for several people to be in it at the same time. One of the circles represents grief, and the other represents joy. Invite the members of the group to explore their own emotions in each of these circles. You may concentrate solely on your feelings about the place or you can make room for feelings of joy and grief in other aspects of your life as well.

Move in and out of each circle as often as you wish, touching your feelings deeply as they emerge. Allow these feelings to shift or strengthen or vanish. You may find that you want to scream or weep or pound the Earth. You may find that you want to dance or shout and kiss the Earth. When you have fully explored the circles, enter the mandorla where the circles intersect. What is it like to be in the place where grief and joy come together? You may wish to leave the mandorla and enter the two outer circles again and return to the center to experience it anew. Allow plenty of time for this exercise. When you feel complete, leave the mandorla and sit outside it until all members of the group have exited.

When the space is empty, make a collective offering of beauty for the place, in the design, where grief and beauty meet.

11. Make a map of place and what it means to the people. We tend to view places that have become wounded as separate from other, healthier places. We see them as impaired beyond remediation or, on the contrary, so in need of remediation that they can't be approached until a plan, money, time, and tools are immediately at hand. As a result, we often avoid these places, even going out of our way so as not to have to encounter them. By making a map of the place, we relocate ourselves there.

With everyone in the group participating, create your map with grasses, pebbles, bottle caps, bark, and other materials you find. Don't try to be an expert cartographer, getting all the details in correct proportion. It doesn't matter if the pond on your map is a lot closer to the hill than it is in real life or if the otter is almost as big as the river it's swimming in. Be sure to include not just features of the land but also elements that are meaningful to the people present. It might be more relevant to include the tree where one member of the group once stood enrapt at the sight of a great-horned owl than to add the barn next to it. Make your map in a leisurely way, so people can share with one another what they're placing on it and why that element is important to them.

12. Hold a grief circle. People are sometimes embarrassed to admit that they feel grief when a place is hurt. Yet when they go to that place and open their hearts to those feelings of loss, they often discover that layers of other, older sorrows are breached and also demand to be released. A grief ritual can provide a safe yet private place for people to express their feelings as they reunite with the place.

Kinde Nebeker created a grief ritual on the shores of Utah's Great Salt Lake. She placed a stone on the sand in each of the four directions and in the middle set a bowl of water. One at a time, participants could enter this special precinct and express whatever feelings of grief arose in them. If someone needed support, that person could raise a hand and Kinde or someone else would step forward and gently place a hand on his or her shoulder. There was no attempt to comfort, offer Kleenex, or stanch the flow of emotions. Some people expressed their grief for the land, some for a personal loss. As people finished their private observances, they washed their hands and face with water from the bowl and returned to the outer circle. After everyone had participated, the group poured the water from the bowl into a shallow rivulet that ran through the sand toward the lake, so that the flushed-out grief could be symbolically borne away.

13. Praise. The Native American writer and teacher Martin Prechtel has written that "Grief is the best friend of Praise, because Praise is a grandiose giver!" The reverse is also true: Praise is the best friend of grief, because praise peers into the dark, deep bin of grief where everything is jumbled together and pulls out individual items, one by one, to bring to the light.

Make a gift of praise as your act of beauty for the place you're attending. Invite each member of the group to come forth, one at a time, and speak out loud to the place, telling it about its beauty. Be specific: praise the delicate scarlet of the penstemon flower, the rippling line of the hills now shorn of trees, the robins that continue to peck over the grass in the lawn of a home destroyed by fire. There may be a few people in the group who feel shy about speaking aloud. For them and for anyone else who has something private to add, reserve a few minutes at the end of the practice for people to make silent offerings of praise to the place.

14. Weave a wreath. Ask everyone in the group to gather flowers, leaves, feathers, and other lightweight materials from around the place. Everyone then sits in a circle with these natural objects in the middle. Using grasses or some kind organic twine that you have brought with you, weave the beauty of the place into a wreath, with everyone adding pieces that are available to all. When you have completed your wreath, offer it to the place with words of gratitude or consolation.

15. Be creative with trash. If you know (or suspect) that your wounded place will be littered with trash, bring along a few large plastic garbage bags when you come for your Earth Exchange. During your event, pick up as much trash as you can. Before you take it away, make something beautiful with it: a RadJoy Bird, an animal or plant whose life in this place has become threatened because of the damage, a beautiful design, or some other work of art. Photograph yourselves with what you've made, then carry out the trash. Be sure to dispose of it in an appropriate place.

16. Meditate. Meditation is a way to bring yourself into the moment, to recognize that all that is within us and around us is constantly shifting, changing, mutable. If you choose to meditate in a wounded place, do so not to remove your consciousness away from the place, but to incorporate the place into you and you into it. You do not need to be a trained meditator to do this. Simply sit down and expand your awareness of the reality of the moment. How does your body feel sitting where it's sitting? How does the air feel on your face and hands? What sounds can you hear? Welcome them. You can even do this practice in a busy, crowded place. When Occupy activists in Oakland, California learned that police were planning to raid their encampment, they began to discuss how they would respond. One man, Pancho Ramos Stierle, decided that, "If police are stepping up their violence, we need to step up our nonviolence." At 6:30 in the morning on the designated day, the police arrived in riot gear, armed with pepper spray and rubber bullets. But instead of angry protestors, they encountered thirty-two people sitting quietly on the street, meditating. The police carried out their orders to arrest people, but the meditators remained peaceful and non-confrontational.[6]

17. Invite other people you meet to be part of your event. It's possible that when you go to your place for your Earth Exchange, you feel a little shy about what you've come to do. Going to a wounded place in order to find and make beauty is not a common response to an environmental problem, after all! You may worry that other people won't understand or might even laugh at you. But since Earth Exchanges are meant for all people who love a place, everyone who meets that simple qualification ought to be welcome—whether they choose to join or not. So, if you arrive at your forest or beach or power plant and encounter others, tell them what you're doing and invite them to be part of the experience. You never know what will happen!

Every year Autumn VanOrd and Lisa McCall do their Global Earth Exchange at Wyman Park in Baltimore. One year they met a young man from the working class neighborhood nearby who had ridden over on his bike to dig worms for fishing. As the two women picked up trash and admired the beauty of this city park, they had periodic conversations with the young man. He talked about how much he had loved coming to the park when he was growing up, but that it had changed for the worse. He said that although he had once found worms easily, now it was harder and the worms were smaller. He never took the small worms, he told them. And he expressed his belief that young kids need to be taught to take care of their environment. "He was very wise and tuned in," Lisa wrote. "Autumn and I felt it was a very timely meet-up."

18. Reach out to the people you associate with the wounding of the place. Besides inviting into your Earth Exchange a person who just happens to be there, reach out to those who work there or whom you hold responsible for what happened to damage the place. Loggers, the man stationed at the entry gate to a power plant, a city official. Get in touch with them before the event or after you arrive. Explain what you're doing there. Tell them an Earth Exchange is not a protest but an occasion for people to share what the place means to them and make a simple gift for it, and that everyone who cares about the place is welcome. They may decline the invitation, but they will be glad that you've asked, and you will be glad that you've expanded the creative possibilities and deepened compassion.

19. Discover through doing it your own knack for guerrilla beauty. When you make beauty for a wounded place, you have no idea who will witness either the act or the outcome. That's the point. You do the thing because doing it is your whole imperative. You give and make no covenants on how your gift will be received.

20. Practice *tonglen*. *Tonglen* is a Buddhist practice that entails taking sorrow into ourselves and sending out relief. It is a way of being in compassionate fellowship with others who are suffering without becoming overwhelmed with suffering ourselves. The rhythm of the practice is the simple rhythm of your breath, with a focus on each inhalation and exhalation. When you breathe in, focus on a group of people or non-human species who are suffering and take in their pain. It is as if you are giving them a

42

tiny bit of relief by sharing the burden. Now, as you breathe out, offer love and relief. You might imagine offering some specific quality such as health, clean air, flowers. Writing of the practice of *tonglen*, Buddhist teacher Pema Chödrön says, "At the relative level, our noble heart is felt as kinship with all beings. At the absolute level, we experience it as groundlessness or open space."[7] One RadJoy member, Mike Beck, described his experience with the practice this way: "In this practice I become a perceptual translator, soaking in one reality and spinning it back, using my breath with a strand of wellbeing that I choose to think becomes part of the fabric of location forever more. It is a tangible conjoining of my inner and outer realities infused with imaginative possibility and care."

21. Give the place part of yourself. We are profoundly and enduringly affected by the places in our lives, whether we have lived there for many years or fallen in love with them during a brief vacation. Part of our grief when the place falls on hard times is related to our sense that the place has died, that it has become irrevocably severed from us—or we from it. As a gift of beauty to your wounded place, leave behind a physical part of yourself to reclaim that relationship. Dig a hole in the ground and place into it a lock of hair, a fingernail paring, your tears, or your spittle. Make this offering mindfully, bearing in mind that it symbolizes the ongoing, intrinsic nature of your connection. Cover the hole carefully and place a stone or flowers on top of it to seal the import of what you have done.

22. Do a vigil. Perhaps you would like to offer your place a gift of extended mindfulness. A vigil is a kind of looking that is different from the studied concentration of a biologist peering into a microscope. Instead, it is expanded, prayerful attention. You can sit a vigil anyplace: at a gas drilling site, a municipal landfill, a demolition site. As always, make sure not to endanger your health and safety: don't trespass or go into a toxic environment. Bring water to drink and perhaps a beach chair or something else to sit on. While you sit, simply watch. Do not distract yourself by reading or checking your phone. Note how the details of the place emerge bit by bit. Note the way your thoughts move—from attention to despair to boredom, back to attention, then slipping on to something else: anger, preoccupation with the small and large events of your life, sorrow. Stay a little longer than you want to.

23. Have a "different kind of protest." Radical Joy for Hard Times events are all about bringing people together to make a gift for a place. They are not protests or demonstrations—although protests and demonstrations are appropriate and effective in many other circumstances. Since an Earth Exchange is the opposite of a protest, you can play with that concept and hold "a different kind of protest." Instead of shouting your demands in the form of a slogan ("Clean our bay! Clean our bay!") in front of a corporate headquarters, invent a new slogan and shout it to the place ("Fish, we love you! You're beautiful !")

For several years a Naropa University faculty member, Christi Strickland, took a group of students to the Valmont coal plant in Boulder, Colorado for their Global Earth Exchange. One year, they were in the midst of their event when a coal-transporting train approached, the railroad crossing gate closed, and cars began stopping on both sides of the intersection. The students recalled other activist visits to the site, when they had lined the streets with signs to demand that the coal-fired power plant be shut down. They decided that this was a different kind of protest, so they began cheering and waving and wishing everyone a good day.

24. Remind the place (and yourself) of its legendary past. The places we love that have been hurt have existed in many forms.

Native Americans and people whose families have lived in one location for many generations have heard many stories about the lives of these places. Some stories are myths from ancient times about how the land came into being, some are legends of remarkable deeds, some are historic. Some belong to the living memory of those who are creating this very Earth Exchange. And of course every place has a geological history millennia long.

Those stories are part of the life of a place, and they have affected how people think about it and behave there. Sometimes the stories are forgotten when the place is damaged. Before you go to a wounded place, do some research about its past. When you arrive, take time to tell one or more of these stories out loud. Tell them not only to the other people present, but to the land as well. In the process you will be reminding the place of its own proud past.

25. Make masks and enact a spontaneous play. Let your place become the stage for a spontaneous expression of your feelings about what has happened there. Each person can choose natural materials from around the site and craft them into a simple mask. The masks might represent an inhabitant of the place, such as a tree or owl or stone, or even the forces—natural or human—that have caused damage to the place. They can also be fanciful creatures like dragons or forest spirits. Don't try to make the masks perfect or "artistic"; just let them symbolize whatever you have chosen in a simple way.

When the masks are finished, have everyone describe the character they've chosen. Now enact these beings: Move into an exploration of how these characters react to their environment: do they walk or crawl, leap or fly? After people have had a few minutes to experiment on their own, start coming together and interacting. The more you move around the place and with one another, the more you will find your voice, your rhythm, and, most of all, your connection with the place.

At the end of your play, have everyone take their masks off and state to the group their own name: "I am Julie." "I am Ted."

26. Apologize to the place. You are probably not personally responsible for what has happened to this place, but as members of a culture that eagerly buys the newest and coolest versions of electronics, loves the freedom of going places in our cars, eats food trucked to our supermarkets from all over the world, and uses paper for everything from studying for a PhD to wiping up spilled milk, we are all responsible for the degradation of lovely places. Therefore, we can all express our personal regrets for what has happened here.

You can make art of your apology. Ask everyone to choose a natural object, such as a leaf, flower, or stone from the land and then form a circle. One at a time, each person speaks aloud their apology or voices their regret, and places the object in the circle. When everyone has spoken, you might rearrange the objects into a more deliberate design, then conclude with a song or prayer.

27. Use your body as the material for your gift. Your body is an adaptable, flexible art material that is available to you at any time and capable of amazing creativity. You can use it to take on the persona of the beings of your wounded place—tree, buffalo, owl, microbe. You can improvise the situation at hand—and how to resolve that situation. For example, you can be a meadow that "dies" and is then "reborn." If you're in a group, you can all lie down on the ground, each person's head at another's feet, to make a line of protection for the place.

At an old-growth forest in British Columbia that had been clearcut three years earlier, Judy Todd lay down in the middle of the logging road in solidarity with the protesters who had performed that same act—in vain—when the loggers first arrived.

She did this for the forest and in solidarity with the people who had loved it so much that they would risk their lives to protect it, knowing that she would have joined them if she had been there at the time.

28. Turn cartwheels. Do acrobatics. Sometimes people think that they have to be solemn and reverent when they go to a wounded place. Not so! Remember that you are here to make a gift to the place. You could even think of your mission as an effort to bring cheer to a place that's having a hard time. So allow yourself to be silly. Turn cartwheels. Do a funny dance. Balance on a log. Tickle a tree stump. Everyone feels better when they laugh.

29. Revel in the impracticality of your gift! When you give a gift to a wounded place, you offer something that would be considered impractical, even useless, by many people. There will be those who'll tell you that what you do doesn't matter. They say you should be planting trees, cleaning up a beach, collecting litter, joining an organization to save the dolphins. What does making a bird or drumming or turning cartwheels have to do with care for a place? Everything! A great gift is not meant to be practical. The literary deconstructionist Jacques Derrida wrote that an element of impracticality is, in fact, an ideal quality of a gift, which ought to be composed of "the extraordinary, the unusual, the strange, the extravagant, the absurd, the mad."[8]

30. Make a shrine. In the past few decades, many people have joined together, often anonymously, in collective mourning by making an impromptu shrine. We saw this phenomenon, for example, after the deaths of Princess Diana and the victims of the Boston Marathon bombing. They spread around the city of New York after the September 11 attacks. They are the crosses and flowers left at roadsides where people have been killed in car accidents. Make a shrine for a place you care about that has fallen. Decorate it with leaves, flowers, branches, and stones. If you make your shrine in an accessible place, you—and perhaps others, strangers, as well—can make further contributions to it when you pass that way again.

31. Ask everyone present to choose one nature being that is inhabiting this place and speak from its point of view. A place is not just a single thing; it is all that spends time there. A place is a hawk, a fly, a pool of water, a blade of grass pushing through concrete, a tree stump, the warm breeze. Ask everyone in the group to choose one being from the place. Then sit in a circle and briefly tell that being's story. What is it like to be this particular life-force living in this place? What did you-as-this-being feel like when your place was damaged? How are you managing now? This practice is taken from Joanna Macy and John Seed's Council of All Beings, a ritual that "serves to help us acknowledge and give voice to the suffering of our world. It also serves, in equal measure, to help us experience the beauty and power of our interconnectedness with all life."9

32. Make a bridge. Often, when a place is hurt, we feel as if it's been cut off from the rest of the community. As Oneida David Powless has expressed it, the place has become "an orphan from the circle of life." You can make a bridge from isolation to reconnection by forming a symbolic bridge. Begin by inviting those present to share their feelings about what's happened to the place and and any sense they might have of being disconnected from it. Then create a bridge together to symbolically reconnect the wounded place with the rest of the neighborhood, the forest, the park, or whatever larger area you feel it's been severed from. Make the bridge with sticks, stones, leaves, flowers. When the bridge is complete, everyone returns to the wounded area and formally makes the journey from woundedness to wholeness. In this way, you are affirming that all places are valued and beautiful parts of the whole.

33. Share your ceremony with another wounded place similar to yours. If you know people in another city or state or in a country halfway around the world who are struggling to cope with a place that's wounded in the same way yours is, band together with them across the miles to create beauty for these places on the same day. Whether the damage is deforestation, mining, wildfire, or anything else, you share a common grief and together you can lighten the suffering for both your own and the other community.

Decide what kind of practice(s) you will do for your event and how you will incorporate each other's event and circumstances into your own. For example, as the people in your group are sharing their stories, you can include the story of the other community. You could face in the direction of that other place and offer them wishes or prayers for recovery, stamina, support, or something else they might need. You can make a RadJoy bird that's "flying" from your place and heading in their direction. Or create a mandala or other symbol that embodies both what has gone wrong in your respective places and what you love about them.

34. Build a fairy village. Children love to create miniature habitats for the "little people" who might just possibly live in the same place they love to explore. We are never to old to play, create, and imagine together. And the fairies, spirits, or invisible ones in a wounded place might be particularly grateful for some attention to their dwelling! Find a spot that feels magical and full of possibilities for architectural creativity. What will the inhabitants need here: houses, a swimming pool, a meeting place, a dancing ground, a school? Whether you are alone, with children, or with other adults, let yourself sink as fully as possible into the magic of losing yourself in play.

49

35. Make beauty for an insect pest. It's tempting to assume that a place is wounded solely because of the aggressive and harmful presence of a certain insect. Lyme ticks can cause serious illness in humans. Bark beetles, wooly adelgids, emerald ash borers and other insects kill trees. Yet these insects harbor no ill will. They aren't deliberately trying to hurt you. Think how you would feel if everyone despised you and wanted to kill you! Reverse the negative energy directed toward an insect in your area by honoring it.

After you've gathered together with friends and family, invite everyone to speak honestly of the harm you feel this insect has done. Then consider the life of the creature, the phases it goes through from larva to adult. Consider that it is surviving here in this place in the only way it knows how to do. Try to find compassion for the insect. You might want to take turns speaking from the point of view of the insect itself. Together, create an image of it using natural materials.

36. Practice balance (Part B). In Section 1, "Getting to Know the Wounded Place," we wrote that two (or more) apparently conflicting emotions can exist within you at one time, and that you can accept both without having to choose one or the other. You can apply this useful practice in a physical way as well. Find an object in your place that is low to the ground—a tree stump, a log, a line you draw in the sand—and then balance on it as if it were a tightrope. If there are no low objects available, simply stand on the ground on one leg like a heron and try to hold your balance. As you do so, reflect on other kinds of balance that you are encountering through this experience. Consider, for example:

✤ how quickly plants and animals return to inhabit places that have been damaged

✳ how your sorrow for what happened to the place is bal-
    anced by surprising visions or sounds of beauty

✳ how beauty can exist even in the midst of destruction

✳ how your presence in the place brings new life to it

37. Explore compassion and responsibility. It's easy to blame
others for damage to a place you care about. This is especially
true when that place is hurt because human error has caused a
chemical leak, oil spill, mine collapse, or other crisis. Yet, few of
us remain unimplicated in the massive use and abuse of technology and consumerism in our society. You can open up to personal responsibility and compassion for others by having a
discussion about the ways that each of us is involved in what
has happened to this and other places. How, for example, does
your lifestyle perpetuate the extraction of fossil fuels? How does
your use of paper necessitate the cutting of trees? How careful
are you with tap water in drought-stricken lands?

Enter into this discussion not to condemn yourself—or others—but rather to broaden your understanding of how we humans got ourselves into this predicament of overuse,
overconsumption, and over-extraction. You might want to find
an area of your wounded place where you can arrange sticks,
stones, or other items that represent those you blame for what
has happened. Do you and those you love belong among them?
If so, add more items. Can you feel compassion for those who
have contributed to what's gone wrong? If so, readjust the sticks
or stones.

38. Visualize the future together. Our intention with the Earth
Exchange practice is to accept wounded places as *they are
now*. However, that acceptance in no way implies that we can't
then band together to bring new life and vitality to this place.

Bring your vision of a new future for your place into your practice.

In Victoria, New South Wales, Australia, Jenny Mitchell and friends created a Global Earth Exchange that eventually led to the reclamation of Jack Madigan Reserve, a small park that had devolved over the decades into a repository for oil containers and a dump. During their Earth Exchange children made chalk drawings on the sidewalk of how they wanted the land to look in future, people tossed flower seeds through the fence to encourage new growth, and a local choir sang songs, including one written especially for the event. They even invited the mayor to attend (she did). This enthusiastic and affirmative expression of public support for the reserve led directly to its reclamation by the city. Two years later, the park reopened, and people returned to plant flowers and bushes and to celebrate together.

39. Re-invent yoga for your place. Many yoga postures, or *asanas,* are inspired by natural beings, such as the tree, the mountain, the crow, and the fish. For your wounded place, invent your own new *asanas* based on what this place is undergoing as a result of its wounding. For example, you might do postures that represent a cut tree, a rig pulling dark black oil from deep in the Earth, a frog species that has vanished, even a bulldozer that has disrupted this place.

40. Make a mandala. A mandala is a circle with designs or images arranged in the center that represent the cosmos. Tibetan Buddhist monks make intricate mandalas of colored sand, often dedicating them to a particular spiritual quality. The artist Daniel Dancer made a mandala called "Wheel for Toxic Man" on a beach in Yucatan, Mexico in which he filled each of four quadrants with trash of a different color—yellow, red, black, and white—that he picked up on the beach. You can make a mandala at your place by filling your circle with objects from the place that represent the trees, mountains, waters, and beings there. Or perhaps your mandala symbolizes the place as you would wish it to be if it could recover fully. Or you can simply use the materials provided by the place to make a beautiful design.

41. Celebrate the fact that when you make a gift to a place, you are only the first artist. Whether your gift is aural, visual, prayerful, or musical, unknown others will soon come along to finish what you've started. Wind, waves, rain, sun, animals, traffic, or other humans will take over where you leave off. This is not a problem; it's the whole point. Your gift is not meant for posterity or to boost an artistic career. It is not about making something perfect, taking credit, signing your name, or restoring your place to its original state. Like any gift, your act of beauty ceases to belong to you once you have offered it.

42. Hold a religious service at the place. Spending time in natural places evokes a feeling of awe and mystery, whether you believe that nature is God's creation or that trees, hummingbirds, and mountains are imbued with their own living spirit. Bring your spiritual beliefs to the wounded place and make it the subject of a special service. Create an altar using an appropriately shaped natural or human-made object you find. Sing hymns or other songs and offer prayers.

When a 600-year-old oak tree that allegedly sheltered George Washington during a picnic lunch began to die, the Presbyterian Church in whose Basking Ridge, New Jersey yard it stood invited the entire community to join a special service to honor and say goodbye to the tree. That focused attention didn't make losing the tree any easier, but it united all those who had appreciated it and helped them accept that death is a part of all lives.

43. Hold a funeral for a place. Honor the place you love by giving it a formal good-bye ceremony, a funeral. Ask people to make "tombstones" or a "coffin" out of cardboard. The "birthdate" you ascribe could begin as far back as another millennium if, for example, you are honoring the life of a mountain, or as recently as last month if you are paying tribute to an African elephant who was killed by poachers. Have everyone wear black or at least a black armband. Then process solemnly with your tombstones and coffin in a public place. If you know a drummer or a bagpiper, ask them to accompany the group as you walk. You might begin at the wounded place and end at city hall, a mall, town square, or other public place. In Charleston, West Virginia, where the landscape is being permanently disfigured by mining techniques that blow the tops off the mountains, a group held a Funeral for the Mountains. As they solemnly processed down the main street at lunch hour, they carried tombstones that bore the names of the eradicated peaks.

44. Make beauty together. Spread it individually. For a workshop she led in Brookfield, Vermont Fran Weinbaum brought flowers, twigs, feathers, ribbons, and other materials and invited participants to use them and other natural objects they found on site to make small, portable tokens of beauty. People made wreaths, mobiles, and other arrangements. Then each person brought the piece they'd made to someplace they considered wounded and placed it there as an offering.

45. Remember the life of the sky. One wounded place that you can honor anytime at any place is the sky. The sky, or the air, is constantly being battered by pollution. In addition, many of the creatures that once flew in large numbers through it have diminished. So lie on your back on the ground and look up. Gaze first at what is there: the quality of the light, the shapes of the clouds, the trees or buildings at the periphery of your vision, any birds or planes you see, or the stars and moon if you do this practice at night. Now reflect on all that is no longer present in the sky or whose decreasing populations inhabit it less frequently: carrier pigeons, condors, honeybees, bats. While still lying on your back, speak aloud to the sky about what is beautiful about it and what you miss.

46. Do T'ai Chi or Qi Gong for the place. T'ai Chi and Qi Gong are Chinese martial arts practices that cultivate balance, stability, resilience, and presence in the moment. If a member of the group knows one of these practices, ask them to do it as a gift to the place in recognition of the balance, stability, and resilience it needs to survive what has happened to it. Those who don't know that particular martial art can follow along as best they can, or they can simply do their own kind of meditative movement. Shortly after terrorist attacks killed 130 people in Paris in November 2015, Andrew Gardner did T'ai Chi at the Place de la République, where impromptu shrines, flowers, and messages encircled the grand central monument. The slow, graceful movements enacted in the midst of a bustling plaza on a gray, overcast day lent to the scene a timeless ritual presence.

47. Make a pickup pilgrimage. Choose a road, a stretch of beach, a park, or other area where you know there's a lot of litter. Bring garbage bags. If you go with a group, have people spread out along the route, so each person has his or her own section to take care of. Every time you pick up a piece of litter, make a point of noticing something beautiful or touching or fascinating nearby. (It might be the other members of the group, engaged with you in this process!) At the end of your trash-cleaning pilgrimage, place all your trash bags together and make a circle around them. Face the bags, then turn around and face the land you've cleared. Take the bags to a place where they will be collected and disposed of properly.

48. Sing along with your wounded place. Listen carefully to the sound the place makes as it lives with its troubles. Now sing along. Don't bother trying to put words to this song. Just make sounds: moaning sounds, bumpy sounds, struggling sounds, confused sounds. At some point (you won't know when in advance!) the sound will likely change, and you will be singing a song of vitality and health to the place.

49. Include friends who can't be with you. If you know people who would like to attend your Earth Exchange but aren't able to join you, ask them to write short messages that they would like you to convey to the place. Bring the messages with you to the place and during your visit—maybe while those present are sharing their feelings about being there—read the messages from the others. You may choose to have one person read all the messages, or you could pass them around, so everyone reads something.

50. Remember that everyone is an artist. When it's time to make your gift of beauty for the place, welcome and appreciate the efforts of one and all. Children, the elderly, the disabled, the artists, the people who think they're not creative, the bold, the shy—ask them all to contribute. It doesn't matter if the work is perfect. What matters is that everyone present is able to give a gift of beauty to the place that matters to them.

51. Thank the place for hosting you. When you leave this wounded place, turn and thank it for holding you and teaching you during your time there. Bow, blow it a kiss, express your gratitude out loud. Whatever you do, acknowledge in some way, that this place has revealed itself to you, and you have received what it offered.

6—

MAKE GUERRILLA BEAUTY FOR...
(...Earth Exchanges for
Specific Situations)

The suggestions for making beauty that are outlined in Chapter 5 are adaptable in many different kinds of places. However, members of the Radical Joy for Hard Times community have found that certain kinds of wounded places lend themselves to certain kinds of attention and gifts. In this chapter we offer suggestions for several specific kinds of circumstances, from making gifts in a clear-cut forest, to attending to a place that is too dangerous to visit in person, to honoring an endangered or extinct animal species.

You will note that among these suggestions there are a few that entail using materials other than those found on site. That's because these places are buildings or because the Earth Exchange occurs completely or partially away from the wounded place itself.

Your Place Is a Clearcut Forest

52. Make altars on the tree stumps. These altars might reflect some aspect of your own life that has been wounded or broken before its time. Or they might be lovely arrangements for the forest made of torn twigs and branches intertwined with wildflowers. Choose the objects for your altar carefully, paying attention to color, shape, symbolism.

53. Find your stump. Have everyone in the group sit on a stump of his or her own. Then meditate together or sing a song to the forest that's gone and yet remains.

54. Imagine yourself a tree. Stand on the stump of a tree that was felled and imagine what it must have been like to have your life suddenly cut down. Where is your life energy now? Is it in the stump or in the branches and trunk and leaves? Share your feelings with others in the group—or with the forest.

55. Tell your tree's life story. Stand or sit on the stump as if you were the tree that it once was, and tell that tree's story. Include significant "events" like the first emergence of the shoot from the ground, a fierce storm, the development of land nearby, etc.

56. Adorn yourself. Dress yourself in the branches and leaves that have fallen to the ground. Play hide and seek with them. Pretend you're the trees and sing your own dirge.

Your Place Is a Building
Slated for Demolition

57. Lay flowers in front of the building. Do this on a regular basis, taking turns with other members of your Earth Exchange group.

58. Write "love notes" to the building stick them on it.

59. Express yourself. Have everyone who lives or works in the building make an image representing their attachment to it—a heart, a tree, a drawing of the outline of the building—and affix it to their windows.

60. Hold hands. Invite all the people who care about the building to gather together and hold hands around it. If that isn't possible, have everyone walk slowly around the entire building, touching it as they move. Ask a musician—a bagpiper or violinist is ideal—to play music for the group as they process together.

Your Place Is a Mining, Gas Fracking, or Other Mineral Extraction Site

61. Fill a hole. Find a hole in the ground and imagine that it goes deep down to the level from which these fossil fuels are being extracted. Fill the hole with flowers, colorful leaves, and other objects of beauty that you find around the place. As you create your gift of beauty, reflect on the ways in which so many invisible aspects of the Earth are as wounded—and as worthy of appreciation—as the visible ones above ground. The group might also want to have a discussion about the parts of themselves that are hidden and mostly unknown to others, yet are vulnerable and can easily be hurt.

62. Get to know the mineral. Have a discussion in your group about the ways in which you yourselves use the fuel that's mined here. Then join together to make an image of that mineral. If your image of what oil or gas looks like is vague, that's all right. The process of creatively imagining this thing that millions of us use and few try to picture is a way of coming into closer contact with it.

63. Include the workers in your Earth Exchange. Mining coal, cleaning out gas fracking trucks, and working on oil rigs is often a dirty and dangerous business. Environmentalists sometimes make the mistake of condemning the workers along with the corporate chiefs who oversee this damage to the Earth. Many of these workers are doing the only jobs that are available to them, and they are taking risks to their health every day. Take turns expressing your compassion and appreciation for them

Your Place Is a Polluted River

64. Weave a wreath of flowers and grasses. Work in silence, focusing as you do on your intention that the waters run clean again and that the aquatic life be restored to health. When the wreath is complete, place it in the river and watch as it makes its way downstream.

For a Radical Joy for Hard Times event called The Ground Beneath Our Hearts, Liz Gold led a ceremony like this for the Animas River in Durango, Colorado. An old mine had collapsed recently, and the tailings had flooded the river, turning it a sickly orange. After the members of the group had placed their wreath of flowers, feathers, and grasses into the river and were watching it begin to flow downstream, they gasped aloud when the currents reshaped the circular wreath into a heart.

65. Give your appreciation directly to the river. It is magical to watch something you've placed in a river be carried downstream on the current, rounding the bends, getting stuck, getting unstuck. It's like the journey of life. It seems to lead from the present to the future. In this exercise you send your good wishes and appreciation into the river, that it can be carried along until it finds a place where it will temporarily come to rest. Everyone chooses a leaf. Standing in front of the river, they "give" this leaf a few words of appreciation, gratitude, or love for the river. They place their leaves into the river and watch the benediction flow onward.

Your Place Is a Sinkhole, Open Pit, or Other Element of the Land Where the Boundaries of the Damage are Clearly Defined

66. Join hands and dance. Circle hands around this wounded place, then sing a song or do a dance. In July 2000, a group near Butte, Montana danced the hula. Dressed in blue sarongs about 150 women and men spread out around the Berkeley copper pit. Their aim was to call attention to the rising levels of toxic sludge that had been filling the 1,800-foot-deep pit since Atlantic Richfield diverted underground pumping systems in 1982. "We are dancing the hula to alert the public to the need to prioritize funding for the cleanup of the pit," said Kristi Hager, the Montana artist and photographer who organized the event. "We want to demonstrate good will for the pit, emphasize the positive, and acknowledge the sacrifice made by the environment and the people to mine the copper here."[10]

67. Frame the place with beauty. Pick wildflowers or bring them from home and decorate the periphery of the area with them. Or toss them into the pit to bring a little beauty to the depths.

You're Honoring an Endangered or Extinct Animal Species

68. Become the animal. Enter into the life force of the animal by taking on its characteristics. Move as the animal would through its landscape. Sing its sounds. Interact with the other humans in the group as members of your flock or herd or pod. Become intimate with the place in your memory and imagination, exploring how the animal lived there.

69. Revive the animal in your hearts. Invite everyone present to share what this particular endangered animal means to them. Then, work together to make an image of the animal, using natural materials you find.

Your Place Is a Natural or Historic Area That Has Been Plowed, Paved Over or "Invaded" to Make Room for Something New

70. Make a diorama of the old place *in* the new place. Gather at the site and take turns talking about it in two ways: (1) describe in as much detail as possible what the missing place looked like, sounded like, smelled like. Where was the spring, where the foxhole, where the place where the deer came to drink? Then (2) describe how this place made you feel, what you loved about it. Make a "diorama" of the place using found materials or your own bodies.

71. Make beauty for the thing you hate. It can be very challenging to live with a shopping mall or electrical transmission tower or other invasive structure that has marred a natural place you care about. Yet, this invader of the space is probably here to stay, and you will either have to make peace with it or spend a long time being angry.

So why not take a small step toward beautifying the ugly, making friends with the hated stranger? Place flowers before it. Sprinkle it with water to "christen" it the way steamship companies did with their new ships. A group in Gandesa, Spain created small offerings of flowers, stones, and ribbons at each of the four corners of an enormous electrical transmission tower that had been installed on one woman's small private farm that ran entirely off the grid.

Your place Is Too Toxic or
Dangerous to Enter

72. Make beauty for the boundary line. If there's a fence around the place, as at a Superfund site or industry that has been shut down, make beauty on the fence. Weave flowers and grasses into it. Write messages to the place on ribbons or scraps of fabric and tie the ribbons on the fence. At a ceremony in New York City after the September 11 attacks, people wrote messages of support for the city on red ribbons and tied them to a chainlink-fence. For weeks afterward, those ribbons fluttered in the breeze, reminding all who passed them that attention and care had been offered here.

73. Make guerrilla beauty from afar. Even though an Earth Exchange typically requires making a physical visit to a wounded place, sometimes that's impossible—or inadvisable. If the place you want to attend to is unsafe—if it's the site of a toxic chemical spill or an event that has left the surrounding environment unstable—you can still make a gift of beauty for it.

One way to do so is to gather at a safe place and together make a three-dimensional map of the wounded place. Use natural materials, such as leaves, twigs, or flowers. Start with how the place looked and felt before it was damaged and then map out what the damaging force—chemical spill, explosion—did to it. Play with the materials you're working with. Rearrange them. Put yourself in the map. "Remove" the wound or shrink it. "Restore" the place.

74. Make a "pathway" to the place. No matter how far away from the place you must gather together to make your gift of beauty, you can make a path to symbolically reconnect it to the rest of the community. Use an organic substance like flour, cornmeal, sand, or soil to draw a line from your gathering place towards the wounded place. You may be able to make this path only a few feet long, or you may have it cover the actual physical distance. Make this pathway slowly and mindfully, focusing on how the damaged place has become cut off, disconnected from the rest of the community, and on your desire that it be restored so that it is once again part of the wholeness and health of the area. You might want to sing songs or drum as you walk.

75. Make birds. Even if you can't physically be at your wounded place, you can make birds out of paper and hang them from a tree or a fence in honor of the place. Hide Enomoto and a group of men and women who were attending his seminar in Osaka made colorful origami birds a few months after the tsunami and nuclear power plant failure that devastated so much of coastal Japan in 2011.

Your Place Has Native Vegetation
That Is Disappearing or Being
Crowded Out by Invasive Species

76. Praise the plant. Whether your locale is woodland or field, desert or mountain, spend some time looking for the plant that is endangered. If you find it, gather the group around it. Have everyone in the group say a few words to the plant about what they admire about it. If you don't find any representatives of that plant, make an image of the plant out of found materials. Then gather around it and tell this symbolic plant what you admire about it. Feel free to speak also of your sorrow that it is under threat. Give some water to the plant or its image.

77. Re-imagine the invasive species. It's been said that weeds are flowers that are simply growing in the wrong place. That's true of any invasive plant. In this Earth Exchange you pay a little homage to the invader, the plant that people can't stand. Alone or with the entire group gathered together, spend time really looking at this plant. Speaking out loud, tell it what you admire about it. Then, speaking as reasonably and calmly as you can manage, tell the plant why you are unhappy with it and how you perceive its particular vitality harming other, once vital plants in the area. (With a plant, as with a person who's doing something you don't like, it's possible to be clear and honest without being abusive!)

Annie Hess of the Eastern Shore of Virginia has done several Earth Exchanges and workshops devoted to offering a new perspective on the invasive wetlands grass, phragmites. They've woven baskets of this tough, indomitable plant, made a walking trail through a thicket of it, picked them and arranged them in a vase for the dining table, and even held a workshop for children to make "phragic wands" with paint, glitter, and feathers.

You're Outside a Business That You Believe Is Doing Harm to Nature or People

78. Practice generosity, not confrontation. Earth Exchanges are inclusive events. Anyone who cares about a place is welcome to attend, whether that person is a farmer, an artist, a hunter, a lumberjack, a genetic engineer, a priest, or a derrickman at an oil well. It is undeniable, however, that there are businesses and corporations in the world that are contributing to many serious ecological and social problems.

If you decide to do your Earth Exchange at such a place, do so not as a confrontation but rather with the intention of making beauty. Whether your gift of beauty is a RadJoy bird, a song, prayers, or anything else, ask participants to offer it with the wish that those who work at this place be mindful of the wellbeing of people and the Earth. Radical Joy for Hard Times events have taken place at coal-fired power plants, gas drilling sites, and even the genetic engineering giant, Monsanto. Standing in front of the Monsanto plant in Grinnell, Iowa ten human rights activists said prayers to the sun, Earth, and the great mystery each holds most sacred. They then scattered native corn on the corporate lawn as a way of infusing some organic beauty into a business that is altering seeds, farming practices, and agricultural traditions around the world.

79. Invite people who work at this business to participate in your event. Explain to them that an Earth Exchange is not a protest but a way of making beauty for a place that's given a lot to humans. (Pay attention to your language! People employed by these enterprises will be more likely to be sympathetic if you speak of the land as "having given a lot" rather than as "wounded.") If they accept your invitation, let them simply be part of the group. Don't ask anything more or less of them than you ask of anyone else. Encourage them to participate in making the gift of beauty. If they don't accept, simply tell them that if they change their mind, they're welcome to join you late. Give them a RadJoy brochure.

You're at a Place Where an Accident or Act of Violence Occurred

80. Honor those who experienced the wounding. If possible, invite one or more of the people who were hurt in the accident to talk about their experience. Ask the others to talk about their experiences or recollections of the event as well. Then make a simple act of beauty for the place. Fran Sorin of Tel Aviv, Israel led a Global Earth Exchange at the Hayakon River, where a young woman flipped over in her skiff and was submerged underwater for five minutes. Miraculously, she survived and was present at the event to tell her story. The others in the group also shared how her accident had affected them. The ceremony concluded with the young woman and her boyfriend tossing flower petals into the river and everyone present joining together to make a bird out of flowers.

81. Have a ceremony of forgiveness for the place. The mine, the curve in the highway, the river are not to blame for being the place where someone you cared about died or was hurt. Speak aloud to the person or people who were hurt and also to the place. Offer prayers, flowers, songs. Touch the land, the road, the river with your hands as a gesture of forgiveness.

82. Take an action to symbolize your willingness to live anew with this place. Sweep it clean with brooms, plant flowers if possible, pick up trash. It's important to recognize that your memories and feelings about what happened here may continue to be part of your encounters with it for a long time. That is natural. On the other hand, by attending to it in this way, you are gently reminding yourself that the place continues to have its own life apart from that painful event.

The Weather Prevents You From Going to Your Wounded Place as Planned

83. Hold your event in two phases. Invite everyone who was planning to attend to the place to gather at someone's home on the day and time you had planned your visit. You can still do most of the practices you would have done at the place. First, take time for people to share their feelings about what has happened to the place. Then, as in Step 3 of the Earth Exchange guidelines, get to know the place by speaking about it. Together craft a gift of beauty and delegate one or more members of the group to take it to the place once the weather clears.

A small group of friends who had worked together to protect a wilderness area in upstate New York that had recently been purchased by a developer were unable to make the journey to the land because of a violent thunderstorm. Meeting at the home of Ann Roberts, they shared their feelings about the land and about what it had been like to work together to protect it. Then they made an impromptu map of the place, commandeering objects from around the living room, as well as their own jewelry and items from pockets and purses to make rocks, hills, and trees. When the storm had abated, they went outside to the yard and collected flowers and grasses. Each person then placed their natural objects on a red cloth, offering as they did so a wish that the land thrive and attract people who would appreciate its natural beauty. On the following day Ann carried the offering, wrapped in the red cloth, to the place herself and laid it on a large rock on behalf of all who had made it.

You've Lost a Favorite Tree or Several Trees in your Own Yard

84. Give what remains of your tree a new life and new purpose. Honor and remember it by turning the stump into an altar. Make a mandala (see #40) on it with flowers, leaves, stones, and sticks. Place bird seed on it for the birds, or nuts for the squirrels and chipmunks. Decorate it with small objects from your home that you care about, perhaps creating a new arrangement every week or every month. Use the stump as your meditation cushion. Plant flowers around it.

85. Make some wild art for the place. Although the gifts of beauty at Earth Exchanges are usually created with materials that you find on the place itself or are at least biodegradable, when there are one or more dead trees on your own home ground, other possibilities arise. Trees, unless they fall or are deliberately moved, can remain noble, indomitable presences long after they have died. So cheer up the trees and yourself as well by decorating them. Adorn them with Christmas tree balls, colorful ribbons that will flutter in the breeze, or even toys. Or paint them. For the one-year anniversary of a tornado that killed 158 people and destroyed much of the town of Joplin, Missouri, artists painted several of the dead trees in bright colors.

The Wounded Place Is Indoors

Sometimes the place that needs your attention isn't outside in the natural world but inside. You may consider it wounded either because of something that happened to the building itself or because of what happened inside it. We have already made suggestions for how to bring beauty to a building that has itself been damaged by fire, storm, or violence, or one that is slated to be torn down.

The suggestions here apply to places where something has happened or continues to happen within the walls of the building that affect the whole place and all those who enter it. For example, people have done Earth Exchanges in a house where the former owners operated a meth lab, a room where many psychotherapy patients had shed tears, and even a cathedral in an English town that was cursed by a sixteenth–century bishop.

86. Bring flowers to the place. No matter what it was that happened to this building, you can always bring color and life to the place—and to the people who use it—by sprucing it up with flowers. Leave small vases of flowers here and there throughout the building or lay individual flowers randomly throughout the space so passersby can pick them up.

87. Write love notes to the place. Ask everyone in the group to write some little love notes for the place—expressions of gratitude, observations of the beauty in the place, things you appreciate. Then hide them for unknown people to discover sometime in the future. The Radical Joy for Hard Times board of directors did this once for the house outside Washington, DC that they had rented for their annual board meeting. Because no one lived in the house full-time and the people who occupied it were always transients, the place felt sterile and un-cared-for. At the end of their weekend meeting, the board members wrote on post-its things they appreciated about the house, greetings to future renters, and expressions of gratitude to the house for hosting them. They stuck these in out-of-the-way places like closets, windowsills, the hot water heater, and in kitchen drawers.

88. Make beauty at ground zero of the place. If possible, concentrate your act of guerrilla beauty at the exact place—or as close as possible—to where the accident or act of violence that hurt this place occurred. Make a shrine, an altar, or a RadJoy bird at this spot. Do it mindfully, perhaps in silence, inviting anyone who was involved, either directly or indirectly, in the wounding event to participate. As you create this work of beauty, play music, read a poem, or speak the name(s) of those who were hurt.

89. Bring beauty and comfort to a hospital or other place where people are ailing. Sometimes a building feels wounded or sick simply because those who are confined to it are wounded or sick. Every day people all over the world bring flowers and cards to those they love who are in the hospital. You can extend this custom by including the place itself in your min-istrations. One particularly imaginative Global Earth Exchange occurred at the bone marrow transplant unit of a large hospital in Tel Aviv, Israel. Because people awaiting this medical proce-dure have extremely fragile immune systems, they are not al-lowed to keep any plants or fresh flowers in their rooms. Yael Hartong Ghera worked with two friends to craft small, fanciful mobiles out of colorful and durable materials. They carried the finished mobiles up to the roof of the hospital, where they at-tached them to long pieces of cord, then dangled them down to the windows in the patients' rooms. Instead of looking at a gray, concrete cityscape, these men and women now had a close-up view of something whimsical and delightful.

7—

KEEPING THE MOMENTUM

It is empowering and uplifting to do an Earth Exchange. People—often people who may previously have believed they had little in common with one another—have come together at a place they all consider damaged or endangered in some way and that they care about. They have shared their personal feelings and experiences about this place and what has happened or is happening to it. They have taken time to get to know the place in its current state. And they have worked together to create a simple gift of beauty for the place, discovering, in the process, that they have also made beauty for themselves and their community.

Now, how do you keep the momentum going? Well, you could wait until the following June, when, once again, people from all over the world will be making beauty for their own wounded places as part of the Global Earth Exchange, and you could join them. Or you could begin cultivating your own practice for making gifts of beauty for places and beings on the Earth. Below are a few examples.

90. Go back to your wounded place on a regular basis. Alone or with friends, return to the place to which you have previously given attention and beauty. Whether you choose to do the five suggested steps of the Earth Exchange or not, be sure to pay attention to how the place has changed since your previous visit. Has the vegetation grown back? Does more or less rubbish litter the ground? What signs of animal and bird life do you notice?

Pay attention, too, to how you feel about the place. What is it like to return? Do you have more or less trepidation about this visit than you did the previous one? Does the place feel different? (Sometimes people who do Earth Exchanges say that the place now feels "loved" or "softened" or even "healed" after it has received some care. Look, too, for your original gift of beauty. What has happened to it since your last visit? How do you feel about what has happened to it? Before you leave, be sure to make a new gift for the place.

91. Return to the wounded place with some or all of the same friends who went with you the first time. As you share how you feel about being there, concentrate on what, if anything, feels different. When you make your new gift of beauty, you may choose to refurbish your previous creation or make an entirely new one.

92. Bring a different friend to your wounded place. When you return to the wounded place you visited before, bring a different friend or family member. Share the practice of the Earth Exchange with them. Talk to them about how they feel about this process and whether or not it has made a difference in how they feel about the place. Make a gift of beauty together.

93. Make gifts of beauty for other wounded places as often as you can. People who have done Earth Exchanges often say that once they've visited one wounded place, gotten reacquainted with it, and made something personal and creative for it, their whole consciousness about wounded places in general undergoes a shift. You may find this to be true for you as well. So start looking for wounded places wherever you go. You may notice that there are a lot more of them, small and large, than you'd imagined. Of course, you can't make beauty for them all, but do be on the lookout for places where you can stop and give some attention. Those small acts of beauty might be:

❋ bowing

❋ moving a dead animal out of the road and covering it with leaves or flowers

❋ offering a prayer

❋ singing a song

❋ making a simple RadJoy bird or other image

❋ blowing a kiss

Even such brief acts of kindness make a difference—certainly to you, perhaps to the place, and maybe even to people who witness what you're doing or come upon your act of beauty later.

94. For one day consider all the wood in your house. Your home is no doubt filled with wood serving many different kinds of functions! Keep an eye out for them: floorboards, cutting board, pencils, bedsteads, chests of drawers, cupboards, and many more. Reflect on the numerous unknown trees that these valued bits of your life have come from. Give thanks to those anonymous, generous trees.

95. Honor the metals. The technology we depend on is composed of metals dredged from the belly of the Earth. Without copper, tin, gold, silver, palladium, and other "rare earth" minerals, we wouldn't have mobile phones, computers, televisions, health care diagnostics, or even green energy resources. These rare earth minerals are found only in a few places in the world. A peculiarity of how they form and where is that they like to stick together in those particular places. For that reason they are very difficult to separate. The people who mine them often work under extremely harsh and difficult circumstances. Take a few minutes—perhaps aided by your technological device—to educate yourself about the components of the technology you depend on. Then, when you turn on that device, give thanks for these metals and minerals and to the men and women who toil to extract them for our convenience.

96. Create an altar for a wounded place. Earth Exchanges, whenever possible, are done in the places themselves, not from afar. However, that is not to say that you can't find ways to honor and remember those places in other ways and in other locations. One way to do so is to create an altar or focal point in your home. Designate a certain table or an area on a bookcase or some other spot as the place where you will set up a focal point of mindfulness for that place. Arrange on it photos of the place before and after it was damaged, leaves or stones from the place, a photo of your act of beauty, love notes to the place, and anything else that evokes your feelings of sorrow, hope, and determination. Spend a few minutes each day in meditation or reflection before this commemorative area.

97. Open yourself to a news story on a subject that tends to upset you. Take in the details. Let yourself imagine what the people described in the story are going through. Imagine yourself in their place. How will you reach out to them? Make a donation? Send a card of condolence? Offer them something they could use? Practice tonglen (#20) on their behalf. At the very least open your heart to these people for a few focused breaths.

98. Reflect on the land beneath the house or apartment where you live. What was there before your building stood on it? What was there before that? Who lived on this ground 100 years ago? 500 years ago? 1,000 years ago? If you don't know, do a little research or just stretch your imagination and try to picture these people, their dwellings, the allure of the place that made them—and you—settle there.

99. Make a practice of loving the unbeautiful. Clarissa Pinkola Estes uses the Inuit story of Skeleton Woman to show how the not-beautiful becomes beautiful when we ourselves make it so. In this tale a woman in the relentless pursuit of an impossible love drowns in the icy ocean. Her bones drift beneath the waves. One day a fisherman feels a tug on his line and pulls it up to find not the big fish he anticipates but the remains of the woman. Appalled by this horrifying catch, he's at first tempted to drop her back into the ocean and get rid of her. But his own pity gets the better of him and he hauls the bones into his boat, then takes them back to his snowhouse, where he carefully lays them out.

By and by the skeleton begins to transform. Flesh swathes the bones, the features emerge. Now the fisherman himself begins to change. He turns into a shaman. He takes up his drum and beats it and tells the skeleton to dance. As she does so, she becomes a whole woman again, fleshy, warm-blooded, sensual. The two of them clasp hands, leap into his drum, and run off together.

Pinkola Estes writes: "To untangle Skeleton Woman is to understand that love does not mean all glimmering candles and increase. To untangle Skeleton Woman means that one finds heartening rather than fear in the darkness of regeneration. It means balm for old wounds. It means changing our ways of seeing and being to reflect the health rather than dearth of soul."[11] Whether or not you can make an act of beauty for the wounded, or the "not beautiful," you can almost always pause to consider its past, present, and future beauty.

100. Reseed. This idea comes from a dream that a woman had the night before she participated in a Global Earth Exchange in an area of Santa Fe National Forest that had been badly burned the previous year by a wildfire. She dreamed that a group of people had come to a wounded place to plant corn. The next day, the Earth Exchange group, led by Liz Gold, decided to enact the dream. Since corn is a crop native to this land and the burned forest is public land, they reasoned that they would not be introducing invasive plants or encroaching on private property.

101. Keep refreshing your gift of beauty. If the wounded place you've attended is in an area that is accessible to many concerned people, invite those who have participated in your Earth Exchange, and others as well, to keep visiting it and tending to it. The more people participate in keeping this place vibrant and lively, the more they and others—known and unknown—will gradually begin to perceive it that way. The gestures people make can be as simple as removing dead flowers from a previous act of beauty and adding fresh ones, reshaping the work if winds and people have put it askew, or bringing fresh water, or as elaborate as rebuilding the gift of beauty with each successive visit.

8—

THE INNER WORK OF
RADICAL JOY FOR HARD TIMES

Radical Joy for Hard Times offers a practice for mending our relationship with wounded places on the land and in our communities. Yet those who have made these spontaneous, collaborative guerrilla gifts of beauty for the places they love often realize that the RadJoy practice quite naturally expands into a path for coping with hurt places in ourselves and our societies as well.

Making guerrilla beauty in your daily life, like doing an Earth Exchange for a place, must begin with a willingness to face whatever it is that is making you suffer. Are you troubled by the illness of a loved one or yourself? A broken heart? Financial difficulties? Is your country in crisis? Whatever it is, do not run from but turn toward your raw feelings of grief, rage, or despair.

You will be amazed to discover that, rather than losing yourself in agony, you find that you are now emptied of fear, projection, and angst about what might be. Instead, you are wide open to the moment. In this refreshing space of honesty and receptivity, you become newly attentive to surprising outbursts of beauty and generosity all around—in nature, in your friends and family, and in stories you hear of others.

The practice, though, is only half complete! You don't stop once you have received these gifts of beauty. Now you extend yourself to give beauty outward. This is not beauty-for-credit. It's guerrilla-style beauty: anonymous, spontaneous, stealthy, and ephemeral. You stretch beyond your personal experience of suffering and reach across the space of separation to give something to another. There are infinite ways to do this: tell another person what you appreciate about him or her, hold the door open for a stranger, let somebody go ahead of you in line, pick flowers for someone you love. If, at any time, you get the impulse to do something beautiful or generous for another, don't resist!

In giving these gifts of beauty, we know joy.

The pattern is simple: Grieve. Open. Receive. Give. Receive.

ACKNOWLEDGMENTS

Thanks to these Earth Exchange hosts for their inspiring practices, which we have included in this book: Glenn Albrecht, Mike Beck, Daniel Dancer, Hide Enomoto, Janet Frangs, Andrea Friedmann with Sebastián and Amanda, Andrew Gardner, Yael Hartong Ghera, Liz Gold, Frank Goryl, Annie Hess, Carolyn Lyday, Lisa McCall, Jenny Mitchell, Dianne Monroe, Kinde Nebeker, Ann Roberts, Fran Sorin, Christi Strickland, Judy Todd, Autumn VanOrd, Iris Weaver, and Fran Weinbaum.

NOTES

1 Stephen Duncombe, *Dream: Re-imagining Progressive Politics in an Age of Fantasy* (New York: The New Press, 2007), 92.

2 There are four fundamental guidelines to practicing council:
   1. Listen from your heart.
   2. Speak from your heart.
   3. Be spontaneous.
   4. Be lean & to the point.
To learn more about council, read *The Way of Council* by Jack Zimmerman and Virginia Coyle (Wilton Manor, FL: Bramble Books, 1996).

3 Nancy Willard, *Testimony of the Invisible Man: William Carlos Williams, Francis Ponge, Rainier Maria Rilke, Pablo Neruda* (Columbia: University of Missouri Press, 1970), 6.

4 Robert Johnson, *Owning Your Own Shadow: Understanding the Dark Side of the Psyche* (New York: HarperCollins, 1991), 97-118.

5 Martin Prechtel, *The Smell of Rain on Dust: Grief and Praise* (Berkeley: North Atlantic Books, 2015), 5

6 Originally published in *Radical Joy Revealed*, March 25, 2015.

[7] Pema Chödrön, *When Things Fall Apart: Heart Advice for Difficult Times* (Boston: Shambhala Publications, Inc., 1992), 90.

[8] Anna Primavesi, "The Preoriginal Gift—and Our Response to It," *Ecospirit: Religions and Philosophies for the Earth*, ed. Laurel Kearns and Catherine Keller (New York: Fordham University Press, 2007), 230.

[9] Joanna Macy, "Joanna's essay on the Council of All Beings, July 2002," http://www.joannamacy.net/resources/deepecology/111-joanna-macy-council-of-all-beings-july2002.html.

[10] George Everett, "Cool Water Hula by the Berkeley Pit," 2002, http://www.butteamerica.com/coolhula.htm.

[11] Clarissa Pinkola Estes, *Women Who Run with the Wolves* (London: Rider, 1992), 144.

Made in the USA
Coppell, TX
09 June 2020